Co-dependency

A Practical and Empowering Guide to Recognizing and
Overcoming the Patterns of Codependency in Your Life:
From the Roots of Childhood Trauma to the Steps of Heal-
ing and Self-Discovery

Cathleen R. Barton

Co-dependency: A Practical and Empowering Guide to Recognizing and Overcoming the Patterns of Codependency in Your Life: From the Roots of Childhood Trauma to the Steps of Healing and Self-Discovery

Table of Contents

01: What is Co-dependency?

Co-dependency is a term used to describe a type of unhealthy and dysfunctional behavior that can occur in relationships. It is characterized by an excessive emotional, physical, and psychological reliance on another person, often to the point where an individual's own needs and desires are neglected or suppressed.

At its core, co-dependency is a pattern of relating to others that is characterized by a lack of healthy boundaries and an inability to be autonomous. It is often rooted in childhood trauma or the experience of growing up in an unhealthy or dysfunctional family system.

There are many different ways that co-dependency can manifest in relationships. Some common characteristics of co-dependent behavior include:

– Putting the needs of others before your own

– Seeking validation and approval from others

– Struggling to make decisions for yourself

– Feeling responsible for the feelings and actions of others

01: WHAT IS CO-DEPENDENCY?

– Difficulty saying "no" or setting boundaries

– Difficulty identifying and expressing your own emotions

– Difficulty with self-care and self-worth

Co-dependency can be harmful to both the individual exhibiting the behavior and the people they are in relationships with. It can lead to feelings of resentment, low self-esteem, and a lack of fulfillment in life. It can also contribute to the development of unhealthy patterns of communication and interaction in relationships.

Co-dependency is often associated with unhealthy relationships, such as those that are marked by codependent behavior, abuse, or neglect. However, it is important to note that co-dependency can also occur in seemingly healthy and functional relationships.

If you think you may be in a co-dependent relationship, it is important to seek help. There are many resources available to support you in recognizing and overcoming co-dependent behavior, including therapy, support groups, and self-help books and materials.

01: WHAT IS CO-DEPENDENCY?

Breaking the cycle of co-dependency can be a challenging process, but it is also an empowering and rewarding journey. By learning to set healthy boundaries, communicate effectively, and prioritize your own needs and desires, you can create more fulfilling and healthy relationships with yourself and others.

There are a few key steps that can be helpful in overcoming co-dependency and building healthier relationships:

– Identify your co-dependent behaviors: The first step in overcoming co-dependency is to become aware of the patterns of behavior that contribute to it. This may involve seeking the help of a therapist or joining a support group, where you can gain insight into your own behavior and how it affects your relationships.

– Set healthy boundaries: Setting healthy boundaries is an important aspect of overcoming co-dependency. This means learning to say "no" when you feel overwhelmed or taken advantage of, and establishing clear limits and expectations in your relationships.

– Practice self-care: Co-dependency can often be fueled by a lack of self-care and self-worth. By taking care of your own needs and developing a strong sense of self, you can become more autonomous and less reliant on others for validation and fulfillment.

– Seek support: Overcoming co-dependency can be a difficult process, and it is often helpful to have the support of others. This can include seeking the help of a therapist or joining a support group where you can connect with others who are also working on overcoming co-dependent behavior.

– Learn healthy communication skills: Developing healthy communication skills can be an important aspect of overcoming co-dependency. This includes learning how to express your own needs and boundaries, as well as how to listen to and respect the needs and boundaries of others.

By taking these steps, you can begin to break the cycle of co-dependency and build healthier, more fulfilling relationships with yourself and others. Remember, overcoming co-dependency is a journey, and it may take time and effort. Be patient with yourself, and remember that seeking help and support is an important aspect of the process.

It is important to note that overcoming co-dependency is a

process that may take time and effort. It is not uncommon for individuals to experience setbacks or relapses along the way. If this happens, it is important to be kind to yourself and remember that recovery is a journey, not a destination.

If you feel like you are struggling to overcome co-dependency, it may be helpful to seek the help of a therapist or coach who can provide guidance and support. Therapy can be a safe and supportive space to explore your feelings, thoughts, and behaviors, and to develop new strategies for coping and healing.

In addition to seeking professional help, there are also several self-care strategies that you can try to help you on your journey of recovery. These may include:

— Engaging in activities that bring you joy and relaxation, such as hobbies, exercise, or spending time in nature

— Practicing mindfulness and other stress-reducing techniques, such as deep breathing, meditation, or yoga

— Seeking support from friends and loved ones who are supportive and non-judgmental

– Seeking out healthy role models or mentors who can provide guidance and inspiration

By incorporating these self-care strategies into your daily routine, you can build resilience, reduce stress, and create a sense of balance in your life.

Ultimately, the key to overcoming co-dependency is to prioritize your own needs and well-being. By learning to take care of yourself, set healthy boundaries, and communicate effectively, you can build stronger, more fulfilling relationships with yourself and others.

It is also important to be mindful of the potential for co-dependent behavior to resurface in the future. This is especially true if you have a history of co-dependency in your relationships or if you are returning to a previous relationship where co-dependent patterns were present.

To reduce the risk of relapse, it can be helpful to:

– Stay connected to a support network, such as a therapy group or a support group for individuals recovering from co-dependency

– Continue to practice self-care and prioritize your own needs and well-being

– Communicate openly and honestly with your partner or loved ones about your needs and boundaries

– Seek additional support if you feel overwhelmed or like you are losing ground in your recovery

By being mindful of the potential for co-dependent behavior to resurface and taking proactive steps to prevent it, you can increase your chances of long-term recovery and build healthier, more fulfilling relationships.

Remember, overcoming co-dependency is a journey that requires patience, self-compassion, and a commitment to personal growth. With time, effort, and the right support, you can break the cycle of co-dependency and create more fulfilling, healthy relationships with yourself and others.

02: The Roots of Co-dependency: Understanding Childhood Trauma

Co-dependency is often rooted in early life experiences, particularly those that occur during childhood. Many individuals who struggle with co-dependent behavior have a history of childhood trauma or grew up in unhealthy or dysfunctional family systems.

Childhood trauma can take many forms, including physical, sexual, or emotional abuse; neglect; household dysfunction; or exposure to other traumatic events. These experiences can have a profound and lasting impact on an individual's development and sense of self, and can lay the foundation for co-dependent patterns of behavior later in life.

One way in which childhood trauma can lead to co-dependency is through the development of unhealthy coping mechanisms. When faced with difficult or overwhelming experiences, children may learn to suppress their emotions or to put the needs of others before their own in order to feel a sense of control or to avoid further harm. These coping strategies may provide some short-term relief, but they can also become ingrained patterns of behavior that continue into adulthood, leading to co-dependent relationships.

Another way in which childhood trauma can contribute to co-dependency is through the development of a negative self-image. Children who have experienced trauma may internalize negative messages about themselves, leading to low self-esteem and a lack of self-worth. This can make it difficult for individuals to assert their own needs and boundaries, leading to co-dependent patterns of behavior.

It is important to note that not everyone who has experienced childhood trauma will go on to struggle with co-dependency. However, it is common for individuals with a history of trauma to be more vulnerable to co-dependent patterns of behavior, and it is important to be aware of this connection.

If you think that your co-dependent behavior may be rooted in childhood trauma, it is important to seek help. Therapy can be a valuable resource for individuals who want to explore their past experiences and work through the challenges that they have faced. With the help of a trained therapist, you can learn to cope with your past in healthy ways and build a more fulfilling and autonomous life.

It is also important to be patient with yourself and to remember that healing from childhood trauma is a journey,
not a destination. It may take time to work through the
challenges that you have faced and to develop new, healthier patterns of behavior. With time, effort, and the right
support, you can overcome the roots of co-dependency and
build a more fulfilling and self-sufficient life.

There are a few key steps that you can take to begin healing
from the roots of co-dependency and childhood trauma:

– Seek therapy: Working with a trained therapist can be a
valuable resource for individuals who want to explore the
impact of their past experiences on their present lives. Therapy can provide a safe and supportive space to process and
work through difficult emotions, and to develop new coping
strategies and patterns of behavior.

– Practice self-care: Taking care of yourself is an important
aspect of healing from childhood trauma. This may involve
engaging in activities that bring you joy and relaxation, such
as hobbies, exercise, or spending time in nature. It may also

involve practicing self-compassion and learning to treat yourself with kindness and understanding.

— Seek support: It can be helpful to have the support of others as you work through the challenges of healing from childhood trauma. This may include seeking the help of a therapist or joining a support group, or simply spending time with friends and loved ones who are supportive and non-judgmental.

— Explore your feelings and thoughts: It can be helpful to spend time exploring your feelings and thoughts about your past experiences. This may involve writing in a journal, talking with a therapist or trusted friend, or participating in activities that allow you to express yourself creatively.

— Learn healthy coping strategies: Developing healthy coping strategies can be an important aspect of healing from childhood trauma. This may include learning how to manage stress and regulate your emotions, or practicing mindfulness and other stress-reducing techniques, such as deep breathing, meditation, or yoga.

By taking these steps, you can begin to heal from the roots

of co-dependency and childhood trauma and build a more fulfilling and autonomous life. Remember, healing is a journey, and it may take time and effort. Be patient with yourself, and remember that seeking help and support is an important aspect of the process.

It is important to recognize that healing from childhood trauma and overcoming co-dependent patterns of behavior is a process that may involve ups and downs. There may be times when you feel like you are making progress, and other times when you feel stuck or overwhelmed. This is a normal part of the process, and it is important to be kind to yourself and to remember that healing takes time.

If you feel like you are struggling to overcome co-dependency or to heal from childhood trauma, it may be helpful to seek additional support. This may involve seeking the help of a therapist or coach, joining a support group, or connecting with others who are also working on overcoming similar challenges.

It can also be helpful to have a plan in place for managing setbacks or difficult emotions. This may involve identifying healthy coping strategies, such as talking with a trusted

friend, engaging in self-care activities, or practicing mindfulness, that you can turn to when you are feeling overwhelmed or triggered.

By being proactive and seeking support when needed, you
can increase your chances of success in overcoming co-dependency and healing from childhood trauma. Remember,
you are not alone, and there are many resources available to
help you on your journey of recovery.

In addition to seeking professional help and support, there
are also a few self-care strategies that you can try to help
you on your journey of healing from childhood trauma and
overcoming co-dependency. These may include:

– Engaging in activities that bring you joy and relaxation:
Taking time to do things that you enjoy can be an important
aspect of self-care and can help you to manage stress and
cope with difficult emotions. This may include hobbies, exercise, spending time in nature, or any other activity that
brings you a sense of pleasure and relaxation.

– Practicing mindfulness and other stress-reducing techniques: Techniques such as deep breathing, meditation, or

yoga can be helpful in reducing stress and promoting relaxation. By taking time to focus on the present moment and your breath, you can cultivate a sense of calm and clarity that can help you to cope with challenging emotions.

— Seeking support from friends and loved ones: It can be helpful to have the support of others as you work through the challenges of healing from childhood trauma and overcoming co-dependency. Surrounding yourself with supportive and non-judgmental people can provide a sense of connection and belonging, and can help you to feel less alone.

— Seeking out healthy role models or mentors: Having someone to look up to or to provide guidance and inspiration can be an important aspect of healing and personal growth. Consider seeking out a mentor or role model who has overcome similar challenges and can offer guidance and support as you work to build a more fulfilling life.

By incorporating these self-care strategies into your daily routine, you can build resilience, reduce stress, and create a sense of balance in your life. Remember, healing from childhood trauma and overcoming co-dependency is a journey that requires patience, self-compassion, and a commitment to personal growth. With time, effort, and the right support, you can create a more fulfilling and healthy life for yourself.

03: Recognizing Co-dependent Behaviors in Yourself and Others

One of the first steps in overcoming co-dependency is to become aware of the patterns of behavior that contribute to it. This can be challenging, as co-dependent behavior is often deeply ingrained and may be difficult to recognize. However, by being mindful of the signs and symptoms of co-dependency, you can begin to identify co-dependent behaviors in yourself and others and take steps to address them.

Some common signs of co-dependent behavior include:

– Putting the needs of others before your own

– Seeking validation and approval from others

– Struggling to make decisions for yourself

– Feeling responsible for the feelings and actions of others

– Difficulty saying "no" or setting boundaries

– Difficulty identifying and expressing your own emotions

– Difficulty with self-care and self-worth

03: RECOGNIZING CO-DEPENDENT BEHAVIORS IN YOURSELF AND OTHERS

If you recognize any of these behaviors in yourself or in someone you are close to, it may be worth exploring the possibility of co-dependency.

It is important to note that co-dependent behavior is often learned through experience, particularly in the context of unhealthy or dysfunctional relationships. If you have a history of co-dependent relationships or grew up in a family system that was marked by co-dependent patterns of behavior, you may be more vulnerable to co-dependency.

If you think that you or someone you know may be struggling with co-dependency, it is important to seek help. There are many resources available to support you in recognizing and overcoming co-dependent behavior, including therapy, support groups, and self-help books and materials.

By becoming more aware of co-dependent behaviors in yourself and others, you can take the first step towards building healthier, more fulfilling relationships. Remember, overcoming co-dependency is a journey, and it may take time and effort. Be patient with yourself, and remember that seeking help and support is an important aspect of the process.

03: RECOGNIZING CO-DEPENDENT BEHAVIORS IN YOURSELF AND OTHERS

There are a few key steps that you can take to begin recognizing and addressing co-dependent behaviors in yourself and others:

— Seek therapy: Working with a trained therapist can be a valuable resource for individuals who want to explore co-dependent patterns of behavior and learn new ways of relating to others. Therapy can provide a safe and supportive space to process and work through difficult emotions, and to develop new coping strategies and patterns of behavior.

— Join a support group: Support groups can be a helpful resource for individuals who are working to overcome co-dependency. These groups provide a space to connect with others who are also struggling with similar challenges, and to learn from each other's experiences and insights.

— Read self-help books and materials: There are many self-help books and materials available that can provide guidance and support for individuals who are working to overcome co-dependent behavior. Reading about the experiences of others and learning about effective strategies for change can be a valuable resource on your journey of recovery.

03: RECOGNIZING CO-DEPENDENT BEHAVIORS IN YOURSELF AND OTHERS

– Practice self-care: Taking care of yourself is an important aspect of overcoming co-dependency. This may involve engaging in activities that bring you joy and relaxation, such as hobbies, exercise, or spending time in nature. It may also involve practicing self-compassion and learning to treat yourself with kindness and understanding.

By taking these steps, you can begin to recognize and address co-dependent behaviors in yourself and others, and build healthier, more fulfilling relationships. Remember, overcoming co-dependency is a journey that requires patience, self-compassion,and a commitment to personal growth. It may take time and effort to identify and address co-dependent behaviors, and there may be setbacks along the way. However, by seeking help and support, practicing self-care, and being patient with yourself, you can increase your chances of success in overcoming co-dependency and building healthier relationships.

It is also important to remember that overcoming co-dependency is not just about changing your own behavior, but also about learning to interact with others in a more healthy and autonomous way. This may involve setting and respecting boundaries, learning how to communicate effectively, and building self-worth and self-confidence.

By taking these steps, you can begin to build healthier, more fulfilling relationships with yourself and others, and create a more fulfilling and self-sufficient life. Remember, you are not alone, and there are many resources available to help you on your journey of recovery. With time, effort, and the right support, you can overcome co-dependency and create a more fulfilling and healthy life for yourself.

Another important aspect of overcoming co-dependency is learning how to set and maintain healthy boundaries. Boundaries are the limits we set in our relationships with others that help us to feel safe and respected. They can be physical, emotional, or mental, and they help us to communicate our needs and desires, and to protect ourselves from being taken advantage of or mistreated.

Setting and maintaining healthy boundaries can be challenging, especially if you have a history of co-dependency or have grown up in a family system that did not model healthy boundaries. However, learning to set and respect boundaries is an important aspect of building healthy, autonomous relationships.

Here are a few tips for setting and maintaining healthy boundaries:

– Identify your needs and values: The first step in setting boundaries is to know what you need and what is important to you. Take time to reflect on your own feelings, needs, and values, and be clear about what you are and are not willing to accept in your relationships.

– Communicate your boundaries: Once you have identified your needs and values, it is important to communicate them to others. This may involve saying "no" when you are not comfortable with a request, or expressing your needs and desires in a clear and direct way.

– Respect the boundaries of others: Just as it is important to communicate your own boundaries, it is also important to respect the boundaries of others. This means listening to and acknowledging the needs and desires of others, and being willing to compromise and negotiate when necessary.

– Practice self-care: Taking care of yourself is an important aspect of setting and maintaining healthy boundaries. This may involve setting aside time for yourself, engaging in activities that bring you joy and relaxation, or seeking the help of a therapist or coach if you are struggling to set and maintain boundaries.

By following these tips, you can learn to set and maintain healthy boundaries in your relationships, and build healthier, more fulfilling connections with yourself and others. Remember, setting and respecting boundaries is an ongoing process, and it may take time and effort to develop healthy habits. Be patient with yourself, and seek help if you need it. With time, effort, and the right support, you can learn to set and maintain healthy boundaries and build stronger, more autonomous relationships.

04: The Costs of Co-dependency: How it Affects Your Relationships and Mental Health

Co-dependency can have a profound impact on an individual's relationships and mental health. It can lead to a range of negative consequences, including:

– Difficulty building and maintaining healthy relationships: Co-dependent behavior can make it difficult for individuals to build and maintain healthy, fulfilling relationships. This may be due to a lack of healthy communication and boundaries, or a tendency to put the needs of others before one's own. As a result, co-dependency can lead to feelings of loneliness, isolation, and frustration.

– Difficulty with self-care and self-worth: Co-dependent behavior can also make it difficult for individuals to take care of themselves and to prioritize their own needs. This can lead to a lack of self-worth and self-esteem, and to feelings of inadequacy and worthlessness.

– Mental health challenges: Co-dependency can also have a negative impact on an individual's mental health. It can lead to increased stress and anxiety, as well as to symptoms of depression. It can also make it more difficult for individuals to cope with challenging emotions and situations, leading to a greater risk of mental health problems.

– Interpersonal conflict: Co-dependent behavior can also contribute to interpersonal conflict and strained relationships. This may be due to a lack of healthy communication and boundary-setting, or to a tendency to put the needs of others before one's own. This can lead to feelings of resentment and anger, and to a lack of trust and emotional intimacy in relationships.

Overall, co-dependency can have a range of negative consequences that can affect an individual's relationships and mental health. It is important to be aware of these potential costs and to take steps to address co-dependent behavior in order to build healthier, more fulfilling relationships and improve overall well-being.

If you are struggling with co-dependency and want to overcome its negative effects on your relationships and mental health, there are a few key steps that you can take:

– Seek therapy: Working with a trained therapist can be a

valuable resource for individuals who want to explore co-dependent patterns of behavior and learn new ways of relating to others. Therapy can provide a safe and supportive space to process and work through difficult emotions, and to develop new coping strategies and patterns of behavior.

– Join a support group: Support groups can be a helpful resource for individuals who are working to overcome co-dependency. These groups provide a space to connect with others who are also struggling with similar challenges, and to learn from each other's experiences and insights.

– Read self-help books and materials: There are many self-help books and materials available that can provide guidance and support for individuals who are working to overcome co-dependent behavior. Reading about the experiences of others and learning about effective strategies for change can be a valuable resource on your journey of recovery.

– Practice self-care: Taking care of yourself is an important aspect of overcoming co-dependency. This may involve engaging in activities that bring you joy and relaxation, such as hobbies, exercise, or spending time in nature. It may also involve practicing self-compassion and learning to treat yourself with kindness and understanding.

By taking these steps, you can begin to address co-dependent patterns of behavior and build healthier, more fulfilling relationships. Remember, overcoming co-dependency is a journey that requires patience, self-compassion, and a commitment to personal growth. It may take time and effort to identify and address co-dependent behaviors, and there may be setbacks along the way. However, by seeking help and support, practicing self-care, and being patient with yourself, you can increase your chances of success in overcoming co-dependency and building healthier relationships.

In addition to seeking professional help and support, there are also a few self-care strategies that you can try to help you on your journey of overcoming co-dependency and improving your relationships and mental health. These may include:

– Engaging in activities that bring you joy and relaxation: Taking time to do things that you enjoy can be an important aspect of self-care and can help you to manage stress and cope with difficult emotions. This may include hobbies, exercise, spending time in nature, or any other activity that brings you a sense of pleasure and relaxation.

— Practicing mindfulness and other stress-reducing techniques: Techniques such as deep breathing, meditation, or yoga can be helpful in reducing stress and promoting relaxation. By taking time to focus on the present moment and your breath, you can cultivate a sense of calm and clarity that can help you to cope with challenging emotions.

— Seeking support from friends and loved ones: It can be helpful to have the support of others as you work to overcome co-dependency and improve your relationships and mental health. Surrounding yourself with supportive and non-judgmental people can provide a sense of connection and belonging, and can help you to feel less alone.

— Seeking out healthy role models or mentors: Having someone to look up to or to provide guidance and inspiration can be an important aspect of personal growth and healing. Consider seeking out a mentor or role model who has overcome similar challenges and can offer guidance and support as you work to build a more fulfilling life.

By incorporating these self-care strategies into your daily routine, you can build resilience, reduce stress, and create a sense of balance in your life. Remember, overcomingco-dependency and improving your relationships and mental health is a journey that requires patience, self-compassion, and a commitment to personal growth. With time, effort, and the right support, you can create a more fulfilling and healthy life for yourself.

It is also important to remember that healing and personal growth is an ongoing process, and it is normal to have ups and downs along the way. If you find that you are struggling to make progress or are feeling overwhelmed, it may be helpful to seek additional support. This may involve talking with a therapist or coach, joining a support group, or connecting with others who are also working on overcoming similar challenges.

By being proactive and seeking help when needed, you can increase your chances of success in overcoming co-dependency and improving your relationships and mental health. Remember, you are not alone, and there are many resources available to help you on your journey of recovery. With the right support and a commitment to personal growth, you can build a more fulfilling and healthy life for yourself.

05: Breaking the Cycle of Co-dependency: Setting Boundaries and Finding Empowerment

Breaking the cycle of co-dependency and finding empowerment can be a challenging but ultimately rewarding process. It involves learning how to set and maintain healthy boundaries, developing a sense of self-worth and self-sufficiency, and building healthier, more fulfilling relationships. While it may take time and effort, the benefits of breaking the cycle of co-dependency are numerous, including increased well-being, improved mental health, and stronger, more fulfilling relationships.

One of the key steps in breaking the cycle of co-dependency is learning how to set and maintain healthy boundaries. Boundaries are the limits we set in our relationships with others that help us to feel safe and respected. They can be physical, emotional, or mental, and they help us to communicate our needs and desires, and to protect ourselves from being taken advantage of or mistreated.

Setting and maintaining healthy boundaries can be challenging, especially if you have a history of co-dependency or have grown up in a family system that did not model healthy boundaries. However, learning to set and respect boundaries is an important aspect of building healthy, autonomous relationships.

Here are a few tips for setting and maintaining healthy boundaries:

– Identify your needs and values: The first step in setting boundaries is to know what you need and what is important to you. Take time to reflect on your own feelings, needs, and values, and be clear about what you are and are not willing to accept in your relationships.

– Communicate your boundaries: Once you have identified your needs and values, it is important to communicate them to others. This may involve saying "no" when you are not comfortable with a request, or expressing your needs and desires in a clear and direct way.

– Respect the boundaries of others: Just as it is important to communicate your own boundaries, it is also important to respect the boundaries of others. This means listening to and acknowledging the needs and desires of others, and being willing to compromise and negotiate when necessary.

– Practice self-care: Taking care of yourself is an important aspect of setting and maintaining healthy boundaries. This may involve setting aside time for yourself, engaging in activities that bring you joy and relaxation, or seeking the help of a therapist or coach if you are struggling to set and maintain boundaries.

By following these tips, you can learn to set and maintain healthy boundaries in your relationships, and build health-ier, more fulfilling connections with yourself and others. Remember, setting and respecting boundaries is an ongoing process, and it may take time and effort to develop healthy habits. Be patient with yourself, and seek help if you need it. With time, effort, and the right support, you can learn to set and maintain healthy boundaries and build stronger, more autonomous relationships.

In addition to setting and maintaining healthy boundaries, finding empowerment also involves developing a sense of self-worth and self-sufficiency. This may involve learning to rely on yourself for validation and support, rather than seeking these things from others. It may also involve practicing self-compassion and treating yourself with kindness and understanding, rather than judging or criticizing yourself.

By building self-worth and self-sufficiency, you can increase your sense of autonomy and self-reliance, and become more resilient in the face of challenges. This can also help you to build healthier, more fulfilling relationships, as you are less likely to rely on others for validation and support, and more likely to be able to stand up for yourself and assert your needs and desires.

Finally, breaking the cycle of co-dependency involves building healthier, more fulfilling relationships with others. This may involve learning how to communicate effectively, setting and respecting boundaries, and building trust and emotional intimacy. By cultivating these skills, you can build stronger, more fulfilling onnections with others, and create a more satisfying and self-sufficient life.

There are a few key strategies that can help you to break the cycle of co-dependency and build healthier, more fulfilling relationships:

05: BREAKING THE CYCLE OF CO-DEPENDENCY: SETTING BOUNDARIES AND FINDING EMPOWERMENT

– Seek therapy: Working with a trained therapist can be a valuable resource for individuals who want to explore co-dependent patterns of behavior and learn new ways of relating to others. Therapy can provide a safe and supportive space to process and work through difficult emotions, and to develop new coping strategies and patterns of behavior.

– Join a support group: Support groups can be a helpful resource for individuals who are working to overcome co-dependency. These groups provide a space to connect with others who are also struggling with similar challenges, and to learn from each other's experiences and insights.

– Read self-help books and materials: There are many self-help books and materials available that can provide guidance and support for individuals who are working to overcome co-dependent behavior. Reading about the experiences of others and learning about effective strategies for change can be a valuable resource on your journey of recovery.

– Practice healthy communication: Effective communication is an important aspect of building healthy, fulfilling relationships. This may involve learning how to express your

needs and desires in a clear and direct way, as well as listening to and acknowledging the needs of others.

By taking these steps and incorporating these strategies into
your life, you can break the cycle of co-dependency and
build healthier, more fulfilling relationships. Remember,
overcoming co-dependency is a journey that requires patience, self-compassion, and a commitment to personal
growth. With time, effort, and the right support, you can
create a more fulfilling and self-sufficient life for yourself.

In conclusion, breaking the cycle of co-dependency and
finding empowerment is a challenging but ultimately rewarding process. It involves learning how to set and maintain healthy boundaries, developing a sense of self-worth
and self-sufficiency, and building healthier, more fulfilling
relationships. While it may take time and effort, the benefits
of breaking the cycle of co-dependency are numerous, including increased well-being, improved mental health, and
stronger, more fulfilling relationships.

There are many resources available to help you on your
journey of overcoming co-dependency and finding empowerment. These may include therapy, support groups,

self-help books and materials, and healthy communication strategies. By seeking help and support, practicing self-care, and being patient with yourself, you can increase your chances of success in overcoming co-dependency and building a more fulfilling and self-sufficient life.

Remember, overcoming co-dependency is a journey that requires patience, self-compassion, and a commitment to personal growth. It may take time and effort to identify and address co-dependent behaviors, and there may be setbacks along the way. However, by seeking help and support, practicing self-care, and being patient with yourself, you can increase your chances of success in overcoming co-dependency and building healthier relationships. With the right support and a commitment to personal growth, you can break the cycle of co-dependency and create a more fulfilling and healthy life for yourself.

It is important to keep in mind that overcoming co-dependency and building healthier, more fulfilling relationships is a journey that requires time and effort, and there may be setbacks along the way. It is normal to feel overwhelmed or unsure at times, and it is important to be patient with yourself and to seek help if you need it.

Here are a few tips to help you stay motivated and on track
as you work to overcome co-dependency and build healthier, more fulfilling relationships:

— Set goals and celebrate small victories: Setting small,
achievable goals can help you to stay motivated and make
progress on your journey of recovery. As you achieve each
goal, take time to celebrate your progress and reward yourself for your efforts.

— Find a support network: Connecting with others who are
also working to overcome co-dependency or who have overcome similar challenges can provide a sense of connection
and support. Consider joining a support group or connecting with a coach or therapist who can provide guidance and
encouragement.

— Practice self-care: Taking care of yourself is an important
aspect of overcoming co-dependency and building healthier,
more fulfilling relationships. Make time for activities that
bring you joy and relaxation, and seek the help of a therapist or coach if you are struggling to cope with difficult emo-

tions.

— Seek out healthy role models or mentors: Having someone to look up to or to provide guidance and inspiration can be an important aspect of personal growth and healing. Consider seeking out a mentor or role model who has overcome similar challenges and can offer guidance and support as you work to build a more fulfilling life.

By following these tips and seeking the right support, you can stay motivated and on track as you work to overcome co-dependency and build healthier, more fulfilling relationships. Remember, overcoming co-dependency is a journey that requires patience, self-compassion, and a commitment to personal growth. With the right support and a commitment to change, you can build a more fulfilling and healthy life for yourself.

06: The Role of Communication in Overcoming Co-dependency

Effective communication is an essential component of healthy, fulfilling relationships, and it can play a vital role in overcoming co-dependency. Co-dependent relationships are often characterized by unhealthy patterns of communication, including codependent behavior, lack of assertiveness, and an inability to express needs and boundaries. By learning how to communicate effectively, individuals can break the cycle of co-dependency and build healthier, more autonomous relationships.

So, what does effective communication look like, and how can it help you to overcome co-dependency?

– Assertiveness: Assertiveness involves being able to express your own needs and desires in a clear and direct way, without being aggressive or submissive. It involves being able to stand up for yourself and your beliefs, and to communicate your boundaries in a healthy and respectful way. Assertiveness can be an important aspect of overcoming co-dependency, as it allows you to express your own needs and desires, rather than relying on others for validation or support.

06: THE ROLE OF COMMUNICATION IN OVERCOMING CO-DEPENDENCY

– Active listening: Active listening involves fully paying attention to what the other person is saying, and making an effort to understand their perspective. It involves asking questions, clarifying, and showing empathy. Active listening can be an important aspect of overcoming co-dependency, as it allows you to better understand the needs and perspectives of others, and to build trust and emotional intimacy.

– Clear and direct communication: Clear and direct communication involves being able to express your thoughts and feelings in a clear and concise way, without being passive or aggressive. It involves being honest and open, and being able to communicate your needs and boundaries in a healthy and respectful way. Clear and direct communication can be an important aspect of overcoming co-dependency, as it allows you to express your needs and boundaries, and to build healthier, more fulfilling relationships.

By incorporating these elements of effective communication into your relationships, you can begin to break the cycle of co-dependency and build healthier, more autonomous connections with others. Remember, effective communication is an ongoing process, and it may take time and effort to develop healthy habits. Be patient with yourself, and seek help if you need it. With time, effort, and the right support, you can learn to communicate effectively and build stronger, more fulfilling relationships.

In addition to assertiveness, active listening, and clear and direct communication, there are a few other strategies that can be helpful in overcoming co-dependency and building healthier relationships:

— Seek therapy: Working with a trained therapist can be a valuable resource for individuals who want to explore co-dependent patterns of behavior and learn new ways of relating to others. Therapy can provide a safe and supportive space to process and work through difficult emotions, and to develop new coping strategies and patterns of behavior.

— Join a support group: Support groups can be a helpful resource for individuals who are working to overcome co-dependency. These groups provide a space to connect with others who are also struggling with similar challenges, and to learn from each other's experiences and insights.

06: THE ROLE OF COMMUNICATION IN OVERCOMING CO-DEPENDENCY

– Practice self-care: Taking care of yourself is an important aspect of overcoming co-dependency and building healthier, more fulfilling relationships. Make time for activities that bring you joy and relaxation, and seek the help of a therapist or coach if you are struggling to cope with difficult emotions.

– Seek out healthy role models or mentors: Having someone to look up to or to provide guidance and inspiration can be an important aspect of personal growth and healing. Consider seeking out a mentor or role model who has overcome similar challenges and can offer guidance and support as you work to build a more fulfilling life.

By incorporating these strategies into your life, you can increase your chances of success in overcoming co-dependency and building healthier, more fulfilling relationships. Remember, overcoming co-dependency is a journey that requires patience, self-compassion, and a commitment to personal growth. With the right support and a commitment to change, you can build a more fulfilling and healthy life for yourself.

In conclusion, effective communication is an essential component of healthy, fulfilling relationships, and it can play a vital role in overcoming co-dependency. Assertiveness, active listening, and clear and direct communication are all important aspects of effective communication that can help you to build stronger, more autonomous relationships.

There are also a number of resources available to help you learn and practice effective communication skills. These may include therapy, support groups, self-help books and materials, and healthy communication strategies. By seeking help and support, practicing self-care, and being patient with yourself, you can increase your chances of success in overcoming co-dependency and building healthier, more fulfilling relationships.

Remember, overcoming co-dependency is a journey that requires patience, self-compassion, and a commitment to personal growth. It may take time and effort to identify and address co-dependent behaviors, and there may be setbacks along the way. However, by seeking help and support, practicing self-care, and being patient with yourself, you can increase your chances of success in overcoming co-dependency and building healthier relationships. With the right support and a commitment to change, you can build a more fulfilling and healthy life for yourself.

It is important to remember that overcoming co-dependency and building healthier, more fulfilling relationships is a journey that requires time and effort, and there may be setbacks along the way. It is normal to feel overwhelmed or unsure at times, and it is important to be patient with yourself and to seek help if you need it.

Here are a few tips to help you stay motivated and on track as you work to overcome co-dependency and build healthier, more fulfilling relationships:

– Set goals and celebrate small victories: Setting small, achievable goals can help you to stay motivated and make progress on your journey of recovery. As you achieve each goal, take time to celebrate your progress and reward yourself for your efforts.

– Find a support network: Connecting with others who are also working to overcome co-dependency or who have overcome similar challenges can provide a sense of connection and support. Consider joining a support group or connecting with a coach or therapist who can provide guidance and encouragement.

— Practice self-care: Taking care of yourself is an important aspect of overcoming co-dependency and building healthier, more fulfilling relationships. Make time for activities that bring you joy and relaxation, and seek the help of a therapist or coach if you are struggling to cope with difficult emotions.

— Seek out healthy role models or mentors: Having someone to look up to or to provide guidance and inspiration can be an important aspect of personal growth and healing. Consider seeking out a mentor or role model who has overcome similar challenges and can offer guidance and support as you work to build a more fulfilling life.

By following these tips and seeking the right support, you can stay motivated and on track as you work to overcome co-dependency and build healthier, more fulfilling relationships. Remember, overcoming co-dependency is a journey that requires patience, self-compassion, and a commitment to personal growth. With the right support and a commitment to change, you can build a more fulfilling and healthy life for yourself.

07: Healing from Childhood Trauma: Techniques and Strategies

Childhood trauma can have a lasting impact on an individual's mental health and well-being. It can manifest as a wide range of physical, emotional, and behavioral symptoms, including difficulty with relationships, low self-esteem, and a lack of trust in others. Healing from childhood trauma is a complex and often difficult process, but it is possible with the right support and strategies.

Here are a few techniques and strategies that may be helpful in healing from childhood trauma:

– Seek therapy: Working with a trained therapist can be a valuable resource for individuals who want to explore and heal from their childhood trauma. Therapy can provide a safe and supportive space to process and work through difficult emotions, and to develop coping strategies and patterns of behavior.

– Practice self-care: Taking care of yourself is an important aspect of healing from childhood trauma. This may involve setting aside time for yourself, engaging in activities that

bring you joy and relaxation, or seeking the help of a therapist or coach if you are struggling to cope with difficult
emotions.

− Connect with others: Connecting with others who have
experienced similar challenges can be a valuable resource
for healing from childhood trauma. Consider joining a support group or connecting with a coach or therapist who can
provide guidance and encouragement.

− Practice mindfulness: Mindfulness involves paying attention to the present moment, without judgment. It can be an
effective tool for coping with difficult emotions and managing stress. There are many resources available to help you
learn mindfulness techniques, including books, apps, and
therapy.

− Seek out healthy role models or mentors: Having
someone to look up to or to provide guidance and inspiration can be an important aspect of personal growth and
healing. Consider seeking out a mentor or role model who
has overcome similar challenges and can offer guidance and
support as you work to heal from your childhood trauma.

07: HEALING FROM CHILDHOOD TRAUMA: TECHNIQUES AND STRATEGIES

By incorporating these strategies into your life, you can increase your chances of success in healing from childhood trauma and building a more fulfilling and healthy life for yourself. Remember, healing from childhood trauma is a journey that requires patience, self-compassion, and a commitment to personal growth. With the right support and a commitment to change, you can build a more fulfilling and healthy life for yourself.

It is important to keep in mind that healing from childhood trauma is a complex and often difficult process, and it may take time and effort to make progress. It is normal to feel overwhelmed or unsure at times, and it is important to be patient with yourself and to seek help if you need it.

Here are a few additional tips to help you stay motivated and on track as you work to heal from childhood trauma:

— Set goals and celebrate small victories: Setting small, achievable goals can help you to stay motivated and make progress on your journey of recovery. As you achieve each goal, take time to celebrate your progress and reward yourself for your efforts.

07: HEALING FROM CHILDHOOD TRAUMA: TECHNIQUES AND STRATEGIES

– Practice self-compassion: Self-compassion involves being kind and understanding towards yourself, especially during difficult times. It involves acknowledging that everyone makes mistakes and experiences suffering, and that it is okay to ask for help. Practicing self-compassion can be an important aspect of healing from childhood trauma, as it can help you to build self-acceptance and resilience.

– Find healthy ways to cope with difficult emotions: Healing from childhood trauma often involves learning how to cope with difficult emotions in healthy ways. This may involve practicing mindfulness, engaging in self-care activities, or finding healthy outlets for stress, such as exercise or hobbies.

– Build a supportive network: Building a network of supportive people can be an important aspect of healing from childhood trauma. Consider reaching out to trusted friends and family members, or connecting with others who have experienced similar challenges.

By following these tips and seeking the right support, you can stay motivated and on track as you work to heal from childhood trauma and build a more fulfilling and healthy life for yourself. Remember, healing from childhood trauma is a journey that requires patience, self compassion, and a commitment to personal growth. It may take time and effort to make progress, and there may be setbacks along the way. However, by seeking help and support, practicing self-care, and being patient with yourself, you can increase your chances of success in healing from childhood trauma and building a more fulfilling and healthy life for yourself.

It is also important to keep in mind that healing from child-hood trauma is not a linear process, and it may involve ups and downs. It is normal to feel a range of emotions as you work through your trauma, and it is important to be kind and understanding towards yourself, especially during diffi-cult times.

It may also be helpful to remember that you are not alone in your journey of healing from childhood trauma. There are many resources and support systems available to help you, including therapy, support groups, and self-help materials. By seeking out the right help and support, you can increase your chances of success in healing from childhood trauma and building a more fulfilling and healthy life for yourself.

07: HEALING FROM CHILDHOOD TRAUMA: TECH-NIQUES AND STRATEGIES

In conclusion, healing from childhood trauma is a complex and often difficult process, but it is possible with the right support and strategies. Techniques such as therapy, self-care, connecting with others, practicing mindfulness, and seeking out healthy role models or mentors can all be helpful in healing from childhood trauma and building a more fulfilling and healthy life for yourself.

It is important to remember that healing from childhood trauma is a journey that requires patience, self-compassion, and a commitment to personal growth. It may take time and effort to make progress, and there may be setbacks along the way. However, by seeking help and support, practicing self-care, and being patient with yourself, you can increase your chances of success in healing from childhood trauma and building a more fulfilling and healthy life for yourself.

Remember, you are not alone in your journey of healing from childhood trauma. There are many resources and support systems available to help you, including therapy, support groups, and self-help materials. By seeking out the right help and support, you can increase your chances of success in healing from childhood trauma and building a more fulfilling and healthy life for yourself.

08: Building a Support System for Recovery

Building a support system is an important aspect of recovery from any challenge, including co-dependency, childhood trauma, or other mental health issues. A support system can provide a sense of connection and belonging, as well as practical and emotional support during difficult times. It can also be an important source of motivation and encouragement as you work to build a more fulfilling and healthy life for yourself.

So, how can you go about building a support system for recovery? Here are a few tips to get you started:

— Identify your needs: The first step in building a support system is to identify your needs. This may include emotional support, practical support, or a combination of both. Think about what you need to feel supported and fulfilled, and make a list of the types of support you are looking for.

— Reach out to trusted friends and family members: Your friends and family can be an important source of support and connection. Consider reaching out to trusted friends and family members to see if they are willing to provide the types of support you are looking for. This could involve having someone to talk to, asking for practical help with tasks or errands, or simply having someone to spend time with.

– Join a support group: Support groups can be a helpful resource for individuals who are working to overcome challenges and build healthier, more fulfilling lives. These groups provide a space to connect with others who are also struggling with similar challenges, and to learn from each other's experiences and insights.

– Seek out a mentor or role model: Having someone to look up to or to provide guidance and inspiration can be an important aspect of personal growth and healing. Consider seeking out a mentor or role model who has overcome similar challenges and can offer guidance and support as you work to build a more fulfilling life.

– Consider seeking professional help: If you are struggling to cope with difficult emotions or to build a supportive network, consider seeking the help of a trained therapist or coach. These professionals can provide a safe and supportive space to explore your feelings and develop coping strategies and patterns of behavior.

By incorporating these strategies into your life, you can build a support system that can help you to recover from challenges and build a more fulfilling and healthy life for yourself. Remember, building a support system is an ongoing process, and it may take time and effort to develop healthy habits. Be patient with yourself, and seek help if you need it. With time, effort, and the right support, you can build a strong and supportive network that can help you to recover from challenges and build a more fulfilling and healthy life for yourself.

Here are a few additional tips for building and maintaining a support system for recovery:

— Be open and honest about your needs: In order for your support system to be effective, it is important to be open and honest about your needs. This may involve communicating your feelings and needs to your friends and family, or seeking out a therapist or coach who can provide a safe and supportive space to explore your feelings.

— Practice gratitude: Focusing on the things you are grateful for can help to shift your perspective and build a sense of connection and appreciation. Consider keeping a gratitude journal or sharing your gratitude with others in your support system.

– Take care of yourself: Taking care of yourself is an important aspect of building and maintaining a support system for recovery. Make time for activities that bring you joy and relaxation, and seek the help of a therapist or coach if you are struggling to cope with difficult emotions.

– Seek out new connections: Building a support system is an ongoing process, and it can be helpful to seek out new connections and opportunities for support. This may involve joining a new group or club, or volunteering your time to help others.

– Remember that it is okay to ask for help: Asking for help is a sign of strength, not weakness. If you are struggling to cope with difficult emotions or to build a supportive network, it is important to remember that it is okay to ask for help. There are many resources and support systems available to help you, including therapy, support groups, and self-help materials.

By following these tips and seeking the right support, you can build and maintain a strong and supportive network that can help you to recover from challenges and build a more fulfilling and healthy life for yourself. Remember, building a support system is an ongoing process, and it may take time and effort to develop healthy habits. Be patient with yourself, and seek help if you need it. With time, effort, and the right support, you can build a strong and supportive network that can help you to recover from challenges and build a more fulfilling and healthy life for yourself.

In conclusion, building and maintaining a support system is an important aspect of recovery from any challenge, including co-dependency, childhood trauma, or other mental health issues. A support system can provide a sense of connection and belonging, as well as practical and emotional support during difficult times. It can also be an important source of motivation and encouragement as you work to build a more fulfilling and healthy life for yourself.

There are many ways to build and maintain a support system for recovery, including reaching out to trusted friends and family members, joining a support group, seeking out a mentor or role model, and seeking professional help. It is also important to be open and honest about your needs, practice gratitude, take care of yourself, seek out new connections, and remember that it is okay to ask for help.

Building a support system is an ongoing process, and it may take time and effort to develop healthy habits. Be patient with yourself, and seek help if you need it. With time, effort, and the right support, you can build a strong and supportive network that can help you to recover from challenges and build a more fulfilling and healthy life for yourself.

It is also important to keep in mind that building and maintaining a support system is an ongoing process, and it may involve making adjustments and changes over time. It is normal to experience ups and downs, and to need different levels of support at different times. It is important to be flexible and adaptable, and to be open to seeking out new sources of support as needed.

Here are a few additional tips for building and maintaining a strong and supportive network:

– Cultivate healthy relationships: Building and maintaining healthy relationships is an important aspect of a supportive network. This may involve setting boundaries, communicating openly and honestly, and showing appreciation and gratitude towards others.

– Practice active listening: Active listening involves paying attention to what others are saying and responding with understanding and empathy. It is an important aspect of building and maintaining healthy relationships, and can help to foster a sense of connection and support.

– Offer support and encouragement: A supportive network is not just about receiving support, but also about giving support and encouragement to others. Consider ways in which you can offer support and encouragement to others in your network, whether it be through words of encouragement, a listening ear, or practical help.

– Seek out new connections and opportunities: Building and maintaining a supportive network is an ongoing process, and it can be helpful to seek out new connections and opportunities for support. This may involve joining a new group or club, or volunteering your time to help others.

By following these tips and seeking the right support, you can build and maintain a strong and supportive network that can help you to recover from challenges and build a more fulfilling and healthy life for yourself. Remember, building and maintaining a support system is an ongoing process, and it may take time and effort to develop healthy habits. Be patient with yourself, and seek help if you need it. With time, effort, and the right support, you can build a strong and supportive network that can help you to recover from challenges and build a more fulfilling and healthy life for yourself.

It is also important to remember that a supportive network is not just about seeking help and support from others, but also about taking care of yourself and building resilience. Building resilience involves developing the skills and coping strategies needed to cope with difficult situations and emotions, and to bounce back from setbacks and challenges. Some strategies for building resilience include:

– Practicing self-care: Taking care of yourself is an important aspect of building resilience. This may involve setting aside time for yourself, engaging in activities that bring you joy and relaxation, or seeking the help of a therapist or coach if you are struggling to cope with difficult emotions.

– Developing a support network: Building and maintaining a supportive network of friends, family, and other trusted individuals can be an important aspect of building resilience. A supportive network can provide a sense of connection and belonging, as well as practical and emotional support during difficult times.

– Seeking professional help: If you are struggling to cope with difficult emotions or to build a supportive network, consider seeking the help of a trained therapist or coach. These professionals can provide a safe and supportive space to explore your feelings and develop coping strategies and patterns of behavior.

– Practicing mindfulness: Mindfulness involves paying attention to the present moment, without judgment. It can be an effective tool for coping with difficult emotions and building resilience. There are many resources available to help you learn mindfulness techniques, including books, apps, and therapy.

– Setting goals and celebrating progress: Setting small, achievable goals can help you to stay motivated and make progress on your journey of recovery. As you achieve each goal, take time to celebrate your progress and reward yourself for your efforts.

By incorporating these strategies into your life, you can

build resilience and increase your chances of success in recovering from challenges and building a more fulfilling and healthy life for yourself. Remember, building resilience is an ongoing process, and it may take time and effort to develop healthy habits. Be patient with yourself, and seek help if you need it. With time, effort, and the right support, you can build resilience and increase your chances of success in recovering from challenges and building a more fulfilling and healthy life for yourself.

It is also important to keep in mind that building resilience is not about being able to handle everything on your own, or about pretending that you don't need help or support. Instead, it is about developing the skills and coping strategies needed to cope with difficult situations and emotions, and to bounce back from setbacks and challenges. This may involve seeking help and support from others when needed, and being open and honest about your needs and feelings.

Finally, it is important to remember that building resilience is not about being perfect or never experiencing setbacks or challenges. It is about developing the skills and coping strategies needed to cope with difficult situations and emotions, and to bounce back from setbacks and challenges. It

08: BUILDING A SUPPORT SYSTEM FOR RECOVERY

is a journey that requires patience, self-compassion, and a commitment to personal growth. With time, effort, and the right support, you can build resilience and increase your chances of success in recovering from challenges and building a more fulfilling and healthy life for yourself.

09: Finding Self-worth and Self-love in Recovery

Finding self-worth and self-love is an important aspect of recovery from any challenge, including co-dependency, childhood trauma, or other mental health issues. Self-worth is a belief in your own value and worth as a person, while self-love is an acceptance and appreciation of yourself, including your strengths and weaknesses. Developing self-worth and self-love can be a challenging process, but it is an important step towards building a more fulfilling and healthy life for yourself.

So, how can you go about finding self-worth and self-love in recovery? Here are a few tips to get you started:

– Practice self-acceptance: Self-acceptance involves accepting and embracing yourself as you are, including your strengths and weaknesses. It is an important aspect of developing self-worth and self-love, and can be challenging for many people, especially those who have experienced trauma or other challenges. One way to practice self-acceptance is to focus on your positive qualities and to remind yourself that it is okay to have weaknesses and to make mistakes.

09: FINDING SELF-WORTH AND SELF-LOVE IN RE-COVERY

– Seek out positive role models and mentors: Having someone to look up to or to provide guidance and inspiration can be an important aspect of personal growth and self-love. Consider seeking out positive role models or mentors who embody the qualities you admire, and who can offer guidance and support as you work to build a more fulfilling and healthy life for yourself.

– Engage in self-care: Taking care of yourself is an important aspect of building self-worth and self-love. This may involve setting aside time for yourself, engaging in activities that bring you joy and relaxation, or seeking the help of a therapist or coach if you are struggling to cope with difficult emotions.

– Practice gratitude: Focusing on the things you are grateful for can help to shift your perspective and build a sense of appreciation and self-worth. Consider keeping a gratitude journal or sharing your gratitude with others in your support system.

– Seek professional help: If you are struggling to cope with difficult emotions or to build self-worth and self-love, consider seeking the help of a trained therapist or coach. These professionals can provide a safe and supportive space to explore your feelings and develop coping strategies and patterns of behavior.

By incorporating these strategies into your life, you can build self-worth and self-love and increase your chances of success in recovering from challenges and building a more fulfilling and healthy life for yourself. Remember, finding self-worth and self-love is a journey that requires patience, self-compassion, and a commitment to personal growth. It may take time and effort to make progress, and there may be setbacks along the way. However, with time, effort, and the right support, you can build self-worth and self-love and increase your chances of success in recovering from challenges and building a more fulfilling and healthy life for yourself.

Here are a few additional tips for finding self-worth and self-love in recovery:

– Seek out new experiences and challenges: Engaging in new experiences and challenges can help you to grow and develop new skills, which can in turn boost your self-worth and self-love. Consider trying new hobbies or activities, or seeking out new opportunities for personal growth and development.

— Practice self-compassion: Self-compassion involves treating yourself with kindness and understanding, rather than judgment or criticism. It is an important aspect of self-love, and can be a powerful tool for coping with difficult emotions and setbacks.

— Set boundaries: Setting boundaries involves establishing clear and healthy limits with others, and taking care of your own needs and well-being. It is an important aspect of self-worth and self-love, and can help you to feel more in control of your life and more empowered.

— Find your passions and purpose: Discovering your passions and purpose can be an important aspect of building self-worth and self-love. Consider what brings you joy and fulfillment, and seek out opportunities to pursue these passions and to make a positive impact in the world.

It is also important to keep in mind that finding self-worth and self-love is not about achieving perfection or never experiencing setbacks or challenges. It is about developing a healthy and positive sense of self-worth and self-love, and about embracing and accepting yourself as you are, flaws and all. It is a journey that requires patience, self-compassion, and a commitment to personal growth.

Here are a few additional tips for finding self-worth and self-love in recovery:

– Seek out supportive relationships: Building and maintaining supportive relationships with friends, family, and other trusted individuals can be an important aspect of building self-worth and self-love. A supportive network can provide a sense of connection and belonging, as well as practical and emotional support during difficult times.

– Practice gratitude: Focusing on the things you are grateful for can help to shift your perspective and build a sense of appreciation and self-worth. Consider keeping a gratitude journal or sharing your gratitude with others in your support system.

– Take care of your physical health: Taking care of your physical health is an important aspect of building self-worth and self-love. This may involve exercising regularly, eating a healthy and balanced diet, and getting enough sleep.

– Seek out new opportunities for personal growth: Personal growth is an important aspect of building self-worth and self-love. Consider seeking out new opportunities for personal growth, such as learning a new skill, taking on a new challenge, or pursuing a new hobby or activity.

It is also important to remember that finding self-worth and self-love is not just about focusing on your own needs and well-being, but also about being a part of something larger than yourself. Engaging in activities and causes that are meaningful to you and that make a positive impact in the world can be an important aspect of building self-worth and self-love. This may involve volunteering your time or resources, or advocating for causes you care about.

– Practice gratitude: Focusing on the things you are grateful for can help to shift your perspective and build a sense of appreciation and self-worth. Consider keeping a gratitude journal or sharing your gratitude with others in your support system.

– Seek out supportive relationships: Building and maintaining supportive relationships with friends, family, and other trusted individuals can be an important aspect of building self-worth and self-love. A supportive network can provide a sense of connection and belonging, as well as practical and emotional support during difficult times.

– Seek out new opportunities for personal growth: Personal growth is an important aspect of building self-worth and self-love. Consider seeking out new opportunities for personal growth, such as learning a new skill, taking on a new challenge, or pursuing a new hobby or activity.

– Engage in activities and causes that are meaningful to you: Engaging in activities and causes that are meaningful to you and that make a positive impact in the world can be an important aspect of building self-worth and self-love. This may involve volunteering your time or resources, or advocating for causes you care about.

It is also important to remember that building self-worth and self-love is not a solo journey. Seeking the help and support of others, whether through therapy, support groups, or other resources, can be an important aspect of building self-worth and self-love. These resources can provide a safe and supportive space to explore your feelings and develop coping strategies and patterns of behavior.

Here are a few additional tips for finding self-worth and self-love in recovery:

— Practice self-compassion: Self-compassion involves treating yourself with kindness and understanding, rather than judgment or criticism. It is an important aspect of self-love, and can be a powerful tool for coping with difficult emotions and setbacks.

— Set boundaries: Setting boundaries involves establishing clear and healthy limits with others, and taking care of your own needs and well-being. It is an important aspect of self-worth and self-love, and can help you to feel more in control of your life and more empowered.

— Seek out new experiences and challenges: Engaging in new experiences and challenges can help you to grow and develop new skills, which can in turn boost your self-worth and self-love. Consider trying new hobbies or activities, or seeking out new opportunities for personal growth and development.

09: FINDING SELF-WORTH AND SELF-LOVE IN RE-COVERY

– Seek out supportive relationships: Building and maintaining supportive relationships with friends, family, and other trusted individuals can be an important aspect of building self-worth and self-love. A supportive network can provide a sense of connection and belonging, as well as practical and emotional support during difficult times.

By following these tips and seeking the right support, you can build self-worth and self-love and increase your chances of success in recovering from challenges and building a more fulfilling and healthy life for yourself. Remember, finding self-worth and self-love is a journey that requires patience, self-compassion, and a commitment to personal growth. It may take time and effort to make progress, and there may be setbacks along the way. However, with time, effort, and the right support, you can build self-worth and self-love and increase your chances of success in recovering from challenges and building a more fulfilling and healthy life for yourself.

10: Navigating Intimate Relationships in Recovery

Navigating intimate relationships can be a challenging aspect of recovery from any challenge, including co-dependency, childhood trauma, or other mental health issues. Building and maintaining healthy and fulfilling intimate relationships requires a strong sense of self-worth and self-love, as well as good communication and relationship skills. It is important to be honest with yourself and with your partner about your needs and boundaries, and to be open to seeking help and support if needed.

So, how can you navigate intimate relationships in recovery? Here are a few tips to get you started:

– Practice self-acceptance: Self-acceptance involves accepting and embracing yourself as you are, including your strengths and weaknesses. It is an important aspect of building self-worth and self-love, and can be challenging for many people, especially those who have experienced trauma or other challenges. One way to practice self-acceptance is to focus on your positive qualities and to remind yourself that it is okay to have weaknesses and to make mistakes.

10: NAVIGATING INTIMATE RELATIONSHIPS IN RE-COVERY

– Communicate openly and honestly: Good communication is an important aspect of any healthy relationship. It is important to be open and honest with your partner about your needs, boundaries, and feelings, and to listen actively to your partner's perspective. Seek out resources, such as therapy or communication workshops, if you are struggling with communication in your relationship.

– Set boundaries: Setting boundaries involves establishing clear and healthy limits with your partner, and taking care of your own needs and well-being. It is an important aspect of self-worth and self-love, and can help you to feel more in control of your life and more empowered.

– Seek out support: If you are struggling to navigate your intimate relationships, consider seeking the help of a trained therapist or coach. These professionals can provide a safe and supportive space to explore your feelings and develop coping strategies and patterns of behavior.

It is also important to remember that building and maintaining healthy and fulfilling intimate relationships is not about achieving perfection or never experiencing setbacks or challenges. It is about developing healthy patterns of behavior and communication, and about embracing and accepting yourself and your partner as you are, flaws and all. It is a journey that requires patience, self-compassion, and a commitment to personal growth.

One way to build and maintain healthy and fulfilling intimate relationships is to practice forgiveness. Forgiveness is an important aspect of building and maintaining healthy and fulfilling relationships. It involves letting go of anger and resentment, and focusing on the positive aspects of your relationship. Practicing forgiveness can be challenging, but it can also be incredibly freeing and can help you to build a more positive and healthy relationship with your partner.

Another way to navigate intimate relationships in recovery is to seek out new experiences and challenges. Engaging in new experiences and challenges can help you to grow and develop new skills, which can in turn boost your self-worth and self-love. Consider trying new hobbies or activities, or seeking out new opportunities for personal growth and development.

Building a strong support network is also an important aspect of navigating intimate relationships in recovery. A strong support network of friends, family, and other trusted individuals can provide a sense of connection and belonging, as well as practical and emotional support during difficult times. Consider reaching out to your support network for help and guidance when you are struggling with your intimate relationships.

Finally, seeking out therapy or coaching can be an effective way to navigate intimate relationships in recovery. If you are struggling to navigate your intimate relationships, consider seeking the help of a trained therapist or coach. These professionals can provide a safe and supportive space to explore your feelings and develop coping strategies and patterns of behavior.

It is also important to remember that building and maintaining healthy and fulfilling intimate relationships requires a commitment to ongoing learning and growth. This may involve seeking out new resources, such as books, workshops, or therapy, to learn more about healthy relationship patterns and communication skills. It may also involve being open to feedback from your partner and other trusted individuals, and being willing to make changes in your behavior as needed.

Here are a few additional tips for navigating intimate relationships in recovery:

– Practice self-care: Taking care of your own needs and well-being is an important aspect of building and maintaining healthy and fulfilling relationships. This may involve setting aside time for yourself, engaging in activities that bring you joy and fulfillment, and seeking out the support you need when you are struggling.

– Seek out new experiences and challenges: Engaging in new experiences and challenges can help you to grow and develop new skills, which can in turn boost your self-worth and self-love. Consider trying new hobbies or activities, or seeking out new opportunities for personal growth and development.

– Build a strong support network: A strong support network of friends, family, and other trusted individuals can provide a sense of connection and belonging, as well as practical and emotional support during difficult times. Consider reaching out to your support network for help and guidance when you are struggling with your intimate relationships.

– Seek out therapy or coaching: If you are struggling to navigate your intimate relationships, consider seeking the help of a trained therapist or coach. These professionals can provide a safe and supportive space to explore your feelings and develop coping strategies and patterns of behavior.

– Seek out healthy role models: Observing and learning from healthy relationships can be a helpful way to develop your own skills and patterns of behavior. Consider seeking out healthy role models, such as friends or family members who have strong and fulfilling relationships, and observing and learning from their communication and relationship patterns.

– Practice gratitude: Practicing gratitude involves focusing on the positive aspects of your life, including your relationships. It can help to shift your perspective and to cultivate a sense of contentment and well-being. Consider starting a gratitude journal or sharing your gratitude with your partner on a regular basis.

– Seek out relationship education: There are many re-

sources available to help you learn more about healthy relationship patterns and communication skills. Consider seeking out books, workshops, or therapy to learn more about
how to build and maintain healthy and fulfilling relationships.

– Practice self-compassion: Self-compassion involves being
kind and understanding towards yourself, especially during
difficult times. It can be helpful in building and maintaining
healthy and fulfilling relationships, as it allows you to be
more understanding and forgiving towards yourself and
your partner.

It is also important to remember that building and maintaining healthy and fulfilling intimate relationships requires
a commitment to ongoing learning and growth. This may
involve seeking out new resources, such as books, workshops, or therapy, to learn more about healthy relationship
patterns and communication skills. It may also involve being open to feedback from your partner and other trusted
individuals, and being willing to make changes in your behavior as needed.

– Practice healthy communication: Effective communication is an important aspect of any healthy relationship. It involves being open and honest with your partner about your needs, boundaries, and feelings, and listening actively to your partner's perspective. Seek out resources, such as therapy or communication workshops, if you are struggling with communication in your relationship.

– Seek out relationship education: There are many resources available to help you learn more about healthy relationship patterns and communication skills. Consider seeking out books, workshops, or therapy to learn more about how to build and maintain healthy and fulfilling relationships.

– Practice forgiveness: Forgiveness is an important aspect of building and maintaining healthy and fulfilling relationships. It involves letting go of anger and resentment, and focusing on the positive aspects of your relationship. Practicing forgiveness can be challenging, but it can also be incredibly freeing and can help you to build a more positive and healthy relationship with your partner.

– Seek out therapy or coaching: If you are struggling to navigate your intimate relationships, consider seeking the help of a trained therapist or coach. These professionals can provide a safe and supportive space to explore your feelings and develop coping strategies and patterns of behavior.

By following these tips and seeking the right support, you can navigate intimate relationships in recovery and build a more fulfilling and healthy life for yourself. Remember, building and maintaining healthy and fulfilling intimate relationships is a journey that requires patience, self-compassion, and a commitment to personal growth. It may take time and effort to make progress, and there may be setbacks along the way. However, with time, effort, and the right support, you can navigate intimate relationships in recovery and build a more fulfilling and healthy life for yourself.

11: Coping with Triggers and Relapses

Triggers and relapses are common challenges that many people face in their journey towards recovery from co-dependency, childhood trauma, or other mental health issues. A trigger is anything that can cause a person to experience a strong emotional or physical reaction, often related to past trauma or negative experiences. A relapse refers to a return to old patterns of behavior or thinking, which can be triggered by certain events or circumstances.

Dealing with triggers and preventing relapses is an important part of the recovery process. Here are a few tips to help you cope with triggers and prevent relapses:

– Identify your triggers: The first step in coping with triggers is to become aware of what triggers you. This may involve reflecting on past experiences and the emotions or circumstances that led to a relapse or negative coping behaviors. Once you have identified your triggers, you can develop strategies for managing them.

– Develop a plan for managing triggers: Once you have identified your triggers, it is important to develop a plan for managing them. This may involve identifying healthy coping strategies, such as seeking support from friends or a therapist, practicing self-care, or using relaxation techniques. It may also involve identifying and avoiding situations or environments that may trigger a relapse.

– Build a strong support network: A strong support network of friends, family, and other trusted individuals can provide a sense of connection and belonging, as well as practical and emotional support during difficult times. Consider reaching out to your support network for help and guidance when you are struggling with triggers or at risk of a relapse.

– Seek out therapy or coaching: If you are struggling to cope with triggers or prevent relapses, consider seeking the help of a trained therapist or coach. These professionals can provide a safe and supportive space to explore your feelings and develop coping strategies and patterns of behavior.

– Practice self-compassion: Self-compassion involves being kind and understanding towards yourself, especially during difficult times. It can be helpful in coping with triggers and preventing relapses, as it allows you to be more understanding and forgiving towards yourself and your limitations.

By following these tips and seeking the right support, you can cope with triggers and prevent relapses in your journey towards recovery. Remember, dealing with triggers and preventing relapses is an ongoing process that requires patience, self-compassion, and a commitment to personal growth. It may take time and effort to make progress, and there may be setbacks along the way. However, with time, effort, and the right support, you can cope with triggers and prevent relapses and build a more fulfilling and healthy life for yourself.

Here are a few more tips for coping with triggers and preventing relapses:

– Practice mindfulness: Mindfulness is the practice of being present in the moment, without judgment. It can be a helpful tool in coping with triggers and preventing relapses, as it allows you to become more aware of your thoughts, feelings, and physical sensations, and to respond to them in a more healthy and balanced way.

– Seek out new experiences and challenges: Engaging in new experiences and challenges can help you to grow and develop new skills, which can in turn boost your self-worth and self-love. Consider trying new hobbies or activities, or seeking out new opportunities for personal growth and development.

– Practice self-care: Taking care of your own needs and well-being is an important aspect of coping with triggers and preventing relapses. This may involve setting aside time for yourself, engaging in activities that bring you joy and fulfillment, and seeking out the support you need when you are struggling.

– Seek out healthy role models: Observing and learning from healthy relationships can be a helpful way to develop your own skills and patterns of behavior. Consider seeking out healthy role models, such as friends or family members who have strong and fulfilling relationships, and observing and learning from their communication and relationship patterns.

– Seek out relationship education: There are many resources available to help you learn more about healthy relationship patterns and communication skills. Consider seeking out books, workshops, or therapy to learn more about how to build and maintain healthy and fulfilling relationships.

It is also important to remember that coping with triggers and preventing relapses is an ongoing process that requires a commitment to ongoing learning and growth. This may involve seeking out new resources, such as books, work-shops, or therapy, to learn more about healthy coping strategies and relationship patterns. It may also involve be-ing open to feedback from your support network and being willing to make changes in your behavior as needed.

Here are a few additional tips for coping with triggers and preventing relapses:

– Practice gratitude: Practicing gratitude involves focusing on the positive aspects of your life, including your relation-ships. It can help to shift your perspective and to cultivate a sense of contentment and well-being. Consider starting a gratitude journal or sharing your gratitude with your part-ner on a regular basis.

– Seek out new sources of support: In addition to your regu-lar support network, there are many other resources avail-able to help you cope with triggers and prevent relapses. These may include online support groups, helplines, and peer support programs. Consider seeking out new sources of support to help you navigate difficult times.

– Practice healthy communication: Effective communication is an important aspect of any healthy relationship. It involves being open and honest with your partner about your needs, boundaries, and feelings, and listening actively to your partner's perspective. Seek out resources, such as therapy or communication workshops, if you are struggling with communication in your relationship.

– Seek out new opportunities for personal growth and development: Engaging in new experiences and challenges can help you to grow and develop new skills, which can in turn boost your self-worth and self-love. Consider seeking out new opportunities for personal growth and development, such as workshops, classes, or volunteer work.

It is also important to remember that everyone's journey towards recovery is unique, and what works for one person may not work for another. It is important to be patient with yourself and to focus on your own progress and growth, rather than comparing yourself to others.

Here are a few additional tips for coping with triggers and

preventing relapses:

– Seek out professional help: If you are struggling to cope with triggers or prevent relapses, consider seeking the help of a trained therapist or coach. These professionals can provide a safe and supportive space to explore your feelings and develop coping strategies and patterns of behavior.

– Practice self-acceptance: Self-acceptance involves being accepting and non-judgmental towards yourself, including your flaws, mistakes, and limitations. It can be helpful in coping with triggers and preventing relapses, as it allows you to be more understanding and forgiving towards yourself and your limitations.

– Seek out new sources of support: In addition to your regular support network, there are many other resources available to help you cope with triggers and prevent relapses. These may include online support groups, helplines, and peer support programs. Consider seeking out new sources of support to help you navigate difficult times.

– Seek out healthy role models: Observing and learning from healthy relationships can be a helpful way to develop your own skills and patterns of behavior. Consider seeking out healthy role models, such as friends or family members who have strong and fulfilling relationships, and observing and learning from their communication and relationship patterns.

– Practice healthy self-care: Taking care of your own needs and well-being is an important aspect of coping with triggers and preventing relapses. This may involve setting aside time for yourself, engaging in activities that bring you joy and fulfillment, and seeking out the support you need when you are struggling.

It is also important to remember that it is normal to have setbacks and challenges in your journey towards recovery. If you do experience a relapse or struggle with triggers, it is important to be kind and understanding towards yourself and to remember that recovery is a journey that involves ups and downs.

Here are a few additional tips for coping with triggers and preventing relapses:

– Seek out support: If you are struggling to cope with triggers or prevent a relapse, it is important to seek out the support you need. This may involve reaching out to your support network, seeking the help of a therapist or coach, or joining a support group.

– Practice self-compassion: Self-compassion involves being kind and understanding towards yourself, especially during difficult times. It can be helpful in coping with triggers and preventing relapses, as it allows you to be more understanding and forgiving towards yourself and your limitations.

– Seek out healthy coping strategies: When faced with a trigger or at risk of a relapse, it is important to have a toolkit of healthy coping strategies to help you navigate the situation. These may include healthy self-care practices, such as exercise, meditation, or spending time in nature, or seeking the support of a trusted friend or therapist.

– Learn from your setbacks: If you do experience a relapse or struggle with triggers, try to view it as an opportunity to learn and grow. Reflect on what led to the setback, and consider what you can do differently in the future to prevent similar challenges.

– Seek out new opportunities for personal growth and development: Engaging in new experiences and challenges can help you to grow and develop new skills, which can in turn boost your self-worth and self-love. Consider seeking out new opportunities for personal growth and development, such as workshops, classes, or volunteer work.

By following these tips and seeking the right support, you can cope with triggers and prevent relapses in your journey towards recovery. Remember, dealing with triggers and preventing relapses is an ongoing process that requires patience, self-compassion, and a commitment to personal growth. It may take time and effort to make progress, and there may be setbacks along the way. However, with time, effort, and the right support, you can cope with triggers and prevent relapses and build a more fulfilling and healthy life for yourself.

12: Building a Fulfilling Life in Recovery

Building a fulfilling life in recovery can be a challenging but rewarding process. It involves exploring your values, goals, and interests, and taking steps to create a life that feels meaningful and fulfilling to you. Here are a few tips to help you build a fulfilling life in recovery:

— Explore your values and goals: Building a fulfilling life in recovery often involves identifying your values and goals, and taking steps to align your life with these values. This may involve exploring your interests and passions, and considering what brings you a sense of purpose and meaning.

— Seek out new opportunities for growth and development: Engaging in new experiences and challenges can help you to grow and develop new skills, which can in turn boost your self-worth and self-love. Consider seeking out new opportunities for personal growth and development, such as workshops, classes, or volunteer work.

— Build and maintain healthy relationships: Strong and supportive relationships are an important aspect of a fulfilling life. Consider building and maintaining healthy relationships with friends, family, and loved ones, and seeking out relationship education or therapy if needed.

– Practice self-care: Taking care of your own needs and well-being is an important aspect of building a fulfilling life in recovery. This may involve setting aside time for yourself, engaging in activities that bring you joy and fulfillment, and seeking out the support you need when you are struggling.

Find ways to contribute to your community: Building a fulfilling life often involves finding ways to give back and contribute to your community. Consider volunteering your time, skills, or resources to organizations or causes that are meaningful to you.

Here are a few more tips to help you build a fulfilling life in recovery:

– Practice gratitude: Practicing gratitude involves focusing on the positive aspects of your life, including your relationships. It can help to shift your perspective and to cultivate a sense of contentment and well-being. Consider starting a gratitude journal or sharing your gratitude with your partner on a regular basis.

– Seek out new sources of support: In addition to your regular support network, there are many other resources available to help you build a fulfilling life in recovery. These may include online support groups, helplines, and peer support programs. Consider seeking out new sources of support to help you navigate difficult times.

– Practice healthy communication: Effective communication is an important aspect of any healthy relationship. It involves being open and honest with your partner about your needs, boundaries, and feelings, and listening actively to your partner's perspective. Seek out resources, such as therapy or communication workshops, if you are struggling with communication in your relationship.

– Seek out new experiences and challenges: Engaging in new experiences and challenges can help you to grow and develop new skills, which can in turn boost your self-worth and self-love. Consider trying new hobbies or activities, or seeking out new opportunities for personal growth and development.

– Practice mindfulness: Mindfulness is the practice of being present in the moment, without judgment. It can be a helpful tool in building a fulfilling life in recovery, as it allows you to become more aware of your thoughts, feelings, and physical sensations, and to respond to them in a more healthy and balanced way.

Here are a few more tips to help you build a fulfilling life in recovery:

– Find healthy outlets for your emotions: It is normal to experience a range of emotions in recovery, including both positive and negative emotions. It is important to find healthy outlets for your emotions, such as through journaling, art, or exercise, rather than turning to unhealthy coping mechanisms like substance abuse or unhealthy relationships.

– Practice self-acceptance: Self-acceptance involves being accepting and non-judgmental towards yourself, including your flaws, mistakes, and limitations. It can be helpful in building a fulfilling life in recovery, as it allows you to be more understanding and forgiving towards yourself and your limitations.

– Seek out healthy role models: Observing and learning from healthy relationships can be a helpful way to develop your own skills and patterns of behavior. Consider seeking out healthy role models, such as friends or family members who have strong and fulfilling relationships, and observing and learning from their communication and relationship patterns.

– Learn from your setbacks: If you do experience setbacks or challenges in your journey towards recovery, try to view it as an opportunity to learn and grow. Reflect on what led to the setback, and consider what you can do differently in the future to prevent similar challenges.

– Practice forgiveness: Forgiveness involves letting go of resentment or anger towards others or yourself. It can be an important aspect of building a fulfilling life in recovery, as it allows you to move forward and to focus on your own growth and well-being. Consider seeking out resources, such as therapy or forgiveness workshops, to help you practice forgiveness.

– Practice gratitude: Practicing gratitude involves focusing on the positive aspects of your life, including your recovery journey. It can help to shift your perspective and to cultivate a sense of contentment and well-being. Consider starting a gratitude journal or sharing your gratitude with your support network on a regular basis.

– Find ways to contribute to your community: Building a fulfilling life often involves finding ways to give back and contribute to your community. Consider volunteering your time, skills, or resources to organizations or causes that are meaningful to you.

– Practice healthy self-care: Taking care of your own needs and well-being is an important aspect of building a fulfilling life in recovery. This may involve setting aside time for yourself, engaging in activities that bring you joy and fulfillment, and seeking out the support you need when you are struggling.

– Seek out new sources of support: In addition to your regular support network, there are many other resources available to help you build a fulfilling life in recovery. These may include online support groups, helplines, and peer support programs. Consider seeking out new sources of support to help you navigate difficult times.

– Practice mindfulness: Mindfulness is the practice of being present in the moment, without judgment. It can be a helpful tool in building a fulfilling life in recovery, as it allows you to become more aware of your thoughts, feelings, and physical sensations, and to respond to them in a more healthy and balanced way.

Practice forgiveness: Forgiveness involves letting go of resentment or anger towards others or yourself. It can be an important aspect of building a fulfilling life in recovery, as it allows you to move forward and to focus on your own growth and well-being. Consider seeking out resources, such as therapy or forgiveness workshops, to help you practice forgiveness.

– Learn from your setbacks: If you do experience setbacks or challenges in your journey towards recovery, try to view it as an opportunity to learn and grow. Reflect on what led to the setback, and consider what you can do differently in the future to prevent similar challenges.

– Seek out healthy role models: Observing and learning from healthy relationships can be a helpful way to develop your own skills and patterns of behavior. Consider seeking out healthy role models, such as friends or family members who have strong and fulfilling relationships, and observing and learning from their communication and relationship patterns.

– Practice self-acceptance: Self-acceptance involves being accepting and non-judgmental towards yourself, including your flaws, mistakes, and limitations. It can be helpful in building a fulfilling life in recovery, as it allows you to be more understanding and forgiving towards yourself and your limitations.

– Practice healthy self-care: Taking care of your own needs and well-being is an important aspect of building a fulfilling life in recovery. This may involve setting aside time for yourself, engaging in activities that bring you joy and fulfillment, and seeking out the support you need when you are struggling.

By following these tips and seeking the right support, you can build a fulfilling life in recovery. Remember, building a fulfilling life is an ongoing process that requires patience, self-compassion, and a commitment to personal growth. It may take time and effort to make progress, and there may be setbacks along the way. However, with time, effort, and the right support, you can build a fulfilling and healthy life

12: BUILDING A FULFILLING LIFE IN RECOVERY

for yourself.

13: Celebrating Your Journey of Healing and Self-discovery

Congratulations on making the brave and courageous decision to embark on a journey of healing and self-discovery! This is no small feat, and it is a testament to your strength and determination.

As you celebrate your progress, it is important to take the time to reflect on the journey you have been on. This may involve looking back on the challenges and struggles you have faced, as well as the moments of triumph and growth.

One way to celebrate your journey is to create a visual representation of your journey, such as a collage or a scrapbook. This can be a fun and creative way to reflect on your journey and to honor the progress you have made. You may also consider sharing your journey with others, such as through writing or art, or by speaking with a trusted friend or family member.

It is also important to celebrate your journey in more tangible ways. This may involve treating yourself to something special, such as a massage or a day out with friends. It is important to remember that you deserve to celebrate your progress and to take care of yourself.

As you celebrate your journey, it is also important to re-member that recovery is an ongoing process. It is normal to have ups and downs, and it is important to be kind and un-derstanding towards yourself when you experience set-backs. Remember, the journey of healing and self-discovery is one of growth and personal development, and it is a jour-ney that you are undertaking for yourself.

As you continue on your journey, remember to be proud of the progress you have made, and to celebrate your journey of healing and self-discovery. You have come a long way, and you deserve to celebrate your journey and all that you have achieved. So, take the time to honor yourself and your journey, and remember to celebrate your progress along the way.

Here are a few more tips for celebrating your journey of healing and self-discovery:

– Practice gratitude: Practicing gratitude involves focusing on the positive aspects of your life, including your recovery journey. It can help to shift your perspective and to cultivate a sense of contentment and well-being. Consider starting a gratitude journal or sharing your gratitude with your support network on a regular basis.

– Seek out new experiences and challenges: Engaging in new experiences and challenges can help you to grow and develop new skills, which can in turn boost your self-worth and self-love. Consider trying new hobbies or activities, or seeking out new opportunities for personal growth and development.

– Seek out healthy role models: Observing and learning from healthy relationships can be a helpful way to develop your own skills and patterns of behavior. Consider seeking out healthy role models, such as friends or family members who have strong and fulfilling relationships, and observing and learning from their communication and relationship patterns.

– Practice healthy self-care: Taking care of your own needs and well-being is an important aspect of building a fulfilling life in recovery. This may involve setting aside time for yourself, engaging in activities that bring you joy and fulfillment, and seeking out the support you need when you are struggling.

– Find healthy outlets for your emotions: It is normal to experience a range of emotions in recovery, including both positive and negative emotions. It is important to find healthy outlets for your emotions, such as through journaling, art, or exercise, rather than turning to unhealthy coping mechanisms like substance abuse or unhealthy relationships.

– Practice self-compassion: Self-compassion involves being kind and understanding towards yourself, especially during difficult times. It can be helpful in building a fulfilling life in recovery, as it allows you to be more understanding and forgiving towards yourself and your limitations.

– Learn from your setbacks: If you do experience setbacks or challenges in your journey towards recovery, try to view it as an opportunity to learn and grow. Reflect on what led to the setback, and consider what you can do differently in the future to prevent similar challenges.

– Practice healthy communication: Effective communication is an important aspect of any healthy relationship. It involves being open and honest with your partner about your needs, boundaries, and feelings, and listening actively to your partner's perspective. Seek out resources, such as therapy or communication workshops, if you are struggling with communication in your relationship.

– Build and maintain healthy relationships: Strong and supportive relationships are an important aspect of a fulfilling life. Consider building and maintaining healthy relationships with friends, family, and loved ones, and seeking out relationship education or therapy if needed.

– Practice forgiveness: Forgiveness involves letting go of resentment or anger towards others or yourself. It can be an important aspect of building a fulfilling life in recovery, as it allows you to move forward and to focus on your own growth and well-being. Consider seeking out resources, such as therapy or forgiveness workshops, to help you practice forgiveness.

– Seek out professional support: It can be helpful to seek out professional support, such as therapy or coaching, to help you navigate your journey of healing and self-discovery. A professional can provide you with guidance and support, and can help you to develop strategies and tools to manage challenges and setbacks.

— Set goals and celebrate your achievements: Setting goals and celebrating your achievements can help to keep you motivated and focused on your journey. Consider setting both short-term and long-term goals, and take the time to celebrate your progress along the way.

— Practice mindfulness: Mindfulness involves being present and aware in the moment, without judgment. It can be helpful in building a fulfilling life in recovery, as it allows you to be more present and engaged in your life and relationships. Consider seeking out resources, such as mindfulness meditation or yoga, to help you practice mindfulness.

— Seek out a supportive community: Building a supportive community of friends, family, and loved ones can be an important aspect of your journey of healing and self-discovery. Consider seeking out supportive communities, such as recovery groups or support groups, to help you connect with others who are on a similar journey.

— Take time for self-reflection: Self-reflection involves taking the time to reflect on your thoughts, feelings, and behaviors. It can be helpful in building a fulfilling life in recovery, as it allows you to gain insight into your own patterns and behaviors, and to make positive changes. Consider setting aside time each day or week for self-reflection, and consider seeking out resources, such as journaling or therapy, to help you practice self-reflection.

– Seek out healthy ways to manage stress: It is normal to experience stress as you navigate your journey of healing and self-discovery. However, it is important to find healthy ways to manage stress, such as through exercise, meditation, or hobbies, rather than turning to unhealthy coping mechanisms like substance abuse or unhealthy relationships.

– Practice self-acceptance: Self-acceptance involves being accepting and non-judgmental towards yourself, including your flaws, mistakes, and limitations. It can be helpful in building a fulfilling life in recovery, as it allows you to be more understanding and forgiving towards yourself and your limitations.

– Seek out new opportunities for personal growth: Personal

growth is an important aspect of building a fulfilling life in recovery. Consider seeking out new opportunities for personal growth, such as through education, hobbies, or volunteering.

– Practice gratitude: Practicing gratitude involves focusing on the positive aspects of your life, including your recovery journey. It can help to shift your perspective and to cultivate a sense of contentment and well-being. Consider starting a gratitude journal or sharing your gratitude with your support network on a regular basis.

– Seek out healthy role models: Observing and learning from healthy relationships can be a helpful way to develop your own skills and patterns of behavior. Consider seeking out healthy role models, such as friends or family members who have strong and fulfilling relationships, and observing and learning from their communication and relationship patterns.

As you continue on your journey of healing and self-discovery, remember to celebrate your progress and to take care of yourself. You have come a long way, and you deserve to celebrate your journey and all that you have achieved. So, take

13: CELEBRATING YOUR JOURNEY OF HEALING AND SELF-DISCOVERY

the time to honor yourself and your journey, and remember to celebrate your progress along the way.

Thank You

As we reach the end of this book, I want to say thanks for reading this book.

I want to get this information out to as many people as possible. If you found this book helpful, I would greatly appreciate you leaving me a review. This helps others find the book as well.

Disclaimer

This document is geared towards providing exact and reliable information in regards to the topic and issue covered. The publication is sold on the idea that the publisher is not required to render an accounting, officially permitted, or otherwise, qualified services. If advice is necessary, legal, financial, medical or professional, a practiced individual in the profession should be ordered.

This information is not presented by a financial or medical practitioner and is for entertainment, educational and informational purposes only. The content is not intended as a substitute for professional medical advice, diagnosis, or treatment. Always seek the advice of your physician or other qualified health care provider with any questions you may have regarding a medical condition. Never disregard professional medical advice or delay in seeking it because of something you have read.

The information provided herein is stated to be truthful and consistent, in that any liability, in terms of inattention or otherwise, by any usage or abuse of any policies, processes, or directions contained within is the solitary and utter responsibility of the recipient reader. Under no circumstances

DISCLAIMER

will any legal responsibility or blame be held against the publisher for any reparation, damages, or monetary loss due to the information herein, either directly or indirectly.